"A series of pr... departures and ... up into illumi...... landscape answering or echoing or at odds with the world around her. The writing pulls you in like mesmerizing fiction or a well-crafted memoir and then holds you with the brilliant poetry of its prose. Paige's wayward and peripatetic past threads through New England, San Francisco, Houston, Phoenix, and Italy, in a journey where she navigates through family breakdowns, addiction and a DWI, the Harris County Jail, hard reassessments of recovery, and her life as a writer and teacher. This is powerful and insightful work, filled with moments of beauty and forgiveness worthy of the journeys which led to its creation." DAVID MURA, AUTHOR OF TURNING JAPANESE, A NEW YORK TIMES NOTABLE BOOK OF THE YEAR AND WINNER OF THE PEN OAKLAND JOSEPHINE MILES LITERARY AWARD

"The title of this masterful collection of prose vignettes says it all: what Alexis Paige is trying to map is not a place at all but a state of mind affected by drug and alcohol abuse, 'that liminal no-place between the dead and the living.' If there is redemption here, it is not heroic or even celebration-worthy because Paige doesn't ask us to lament her stumbles or to salute her triumphs. The writing itself—superbly crafted—demands that we pay attention instead to the small labors that might finally lead any of us away from precariously bad choices. Compassionate and clear-eyed, Paige also immerses us in the social and racial injustices that can, in the end, make even those laborious choices futile. At times startlingly poetic about the crude and matter of fact about the breath-taking, Paige manages tone with such deftness we end up more interested in how she thinks than in what she does. She is, in other words, more than a survivor of dangerously hard times; she is a writer to be heralded." BARBARA HURD, WINNER OF THREE PUSHCART PRIZES, AND 2015 GUGGENHEIM FELLOW

ABOUT THE AUTHOR

Alexis Paige's work appears in multiple journals and anthologies, including *Fourth Genre*, *The Pinch*, *The Rumpus*, *Pithead Chapel*, and *Brevity*, where she is an Assistant Editor. Her essay, 'The Right to Remain,' was named a notable in the 2016 *Best American Essays* anthology, was featured on *Longform*, and nominated for a Pushcart Prize. Winner of the 2013 New Millennium Writings Nonfiction Prize, Paige is a graduate of the Stonecoast MFA program. She writes from a converted farmhouse pantry in rural Vermont, where she lives with her husband, and their two dogs, Jazz and George.

Visit Alexis online: *alexispaigewrites.com*

Not A Place On Any Map
Copyright © 2016 Alexis Paige
All rights reserved.

Print Edition
ISBN: 978-1-925417-20-3

Published by Vine Leaves Press 2016
Melbourne, Victoria, Australia

Cover photography © Alexis Paige
Cover design by Jessica Bell
Interior design by Amie McCracken

National Library of Australia Cataloguing-in-Publication entry (pbk)
Creator: Paige, Alexis, author.
Title: Not a place on any map / Alexis Paige.
ISBN: 9781925417203 (paperback)
Subjects: Paige, Alexis--Literary collections.
Essays.
Psychic trauma--Literary collections.
Psychic trauma in literature.
Dewey Number: 824.92

NOT A PLACE ON ANY MAP

ALEXIS PAIGE

Vine Leaves Press
Melbourne, Vic, Australia

CONTENTS

For Fiona.

And for all the survivors of sexual violence.
I believe you. I believe in you.

"It is not down on any map; true places never are."
Herman Melville, *Moby Dick*

AN AUTOBIOGRAPHY OF ARRIVALS

West.

From Phoenix, Los Angeles is a straight shot west on I-10, through nothingness and towns like Blythe, the capital of nothing, then past Joshua Tree and through Palm Springs. The mountains crack out of the shimmering desert floor, and I hold my breath and watch the menace streak by— my small body coiled in the back seat of the station wagon. We are on the run from some apprehension of Mom's, and therefore our own, and the desert floor is a place to bank time, to blast Carole King or Carly Simon and sing loudly about the special vanity of men. It's my brother, 2; me, 6; and Mom, 30, en route to Dad's sister's in Yorba Linda. With Dad gone back east now, our house in Phoenix is stock-still and this is our closest family.

We leave around noon and drive through the mirages until dusk, with Mom singing softly and pulling on her Benson and Hedges 100's. The relief and adrenaline collect here, high in the San Gorgonio pass where the lights of Greater Los Angeles wink through the twisting canyons. With each switchback, the winks pulse steadier, the Pointer Sisters come on the radio, and Mom cranks the dial. She draws deeply on her slim cigarette, and flashes me a wide grin: "I'm so excited! I just can't hide it!" she sings and shimmies into the seat's velour. She knocks her wooden sandals on the brake pedal in time with the bass line as we slide around the next curve. Even I forget myself, forget to fret or be watchful. I dissolve into the show, and for a moment, I am just liquid sequins, hip action, and perfectly-timed snaps. Josh kicks and giggles from his car seat in the back, and the canyon is a cradle of happiness.

I never loved anyone like I loved Mom when she was in bloom. And I never feared anything like I feared her moods.

South.

Arriving in Texas is no thing of ceremony, unless the plane punches through summer storms and lands under bruise-black anvils, but even then the thrill is fleeting. Mostly I feel numb as Houston makes its slow, dumb approach. The city grows closer without drama, its ugliness a fact. Mom lives here now with a boyfriend, a "big job," and her own life, while Josh and I live back in New Hampshire with Dad.

I am maybe nine or ten and will be put on a diet as soon as she sees me. My body likes itself rounder than my small frame, but I am chubbier than usual. I eat my tears, homework, insults, and fear. Striking and slim, Mom fears my weakness. On the ride from the airport, I pray she won't wield the bathroom scale, hold the numbers against me. But ours is a delicate ecosystem.

I stand on the scale, with Mom's perfume suffocating me and her French nail tips on my shoulders. Eighty-six. "You have to lose some weight, kiddo."

And all summer that's what I do. She pinches me here or there and I swim more laps at day camp. For bag lunches, she packs liverwurst on rice cakes and Crystal Lite for me, and Oatmeal Cream Pies and PB & Js on soft bread for Josh. She says, "Don't make a pig of yourself."

I drop weight fast, become tan and almost lithe from the

swimming. We go shopping, and Mom picks out mother-daughter outfits—hunter green shorts and white Henley t-shirts. She curls my hair and fusses and we wear the outfits "out on the town" together, as if in celebration. In the photograph from that outing, we are jutting out our hips and extending the same leg. Mom's smile devours half the frame, and there is a glint of something in her eyes—a moment of light caught in the slipstream—that might as well be happiness. In composition I am doing everything right—my leg extension, my head tilt and calculated side smile, but there is nothing in my eyes. My light is wrong.

North.

Returning to the Northeast, the atmosphere changes, molecules reorder into a recognizable form, and I start to breathe deeply somewhere over Pennsylvania at 30,000 feet. Except on rare clear days—either in winter with high pressure aloft and cerulean skies zinging head-long out every window of the plane, or on lucky days in fall or spring—New England sulks under low clouds.

It's always bumpy on descent into Logan. I watch out the window as cumulus clouds swallow the wing, and then spit it out, and again. The plane bobs along cartoonish puffs of white, and I feel Boston before I see it. We're flying low enough now for the gravity of this place to grab hold—the history, family, the forested nubs and sardined houses, the warm claustrophobia. On final approach, the jet's shadow grazes the tenements of East Boston and then tickles the green-black ink of the harbour. Josh and I grab hands and squeal. We seem to skim the water for a moment, hovering and about to plunge, but then SLAM!, we are down.

We are still young enough that Dad will be waiting, not at baggage claim, but at the gatehouse. His gangly frame and crooked smile rise from a sea of red faces, and we hustle down the jet way, toward home.

West.

San Francisco and Boston are similar arrivals. I am travelling alone now, returning from a bachelorette in Vegas or a wedding back east or a visit here or there. On approach the plane seems about to crash into the bay out near the old Candlestick Park, but just as I brace the armrests and hold my breath, a landing strip appears under the aircraft's belly, and then we are slowing hard on the short runway.

It's the West, not Texas or Boston, and I am without history here. I am 23 or 25, and San Francisco is all mine to fuck up.

True North.

And now I am on the run from the mundane. Vermont is beautiful. I remind myself of this often, as a long ridgeline hums toward the car and my mind puzzles out some work detail or chore. Occasionally, weather will pass through and change the light in the dining room, and this excites me. Snow dances around the room's turret, and I am a snow globe figurine—happy and faceless. I am much older now, and without the same giddy voodoo of my child mind.

But flight still flutters through me, fantasy still thrills me, and the arrivals have plenty of magic still to give.

FINDING YOUR WAY BACK

The canal path in the old mill town, water creeping toward the quarry / awful hollow. Sheets shear from the granite face of the dam, flashes alongside the moon. And, are they insight? Are they headed toward that path you call home?

Into the clearing among the maples and the birches, which sing white. Pines on the outskirts of consciousness, bristling their demands. Each time you jog toward the clear water that runs after the dam. Combing for clarity. Or purity.

In dreams, a mirage you almost reach. But you were there. Are nearly. *Did you ever lose yourself?* he asks. But you are too busy looking. Your hands stone from the April cold of the river. Plunged under. Holding something enormous in the deep, the kaleidoscopic fish dancing on flecked mica. Washing until the waters run clear.

THE RED LINE, BOSTON, MASSACHUSETTS, 1989

Follow her around with a mop, pray for still skies. Pour and clean and tiptoe, and sorry—let me wipe that up, Mom.

Wrung out from playing along, from eyeballing my little brother as he plants his fat feet on a bar stool to reach the counter-top, as Mom shows him how to measure the booze and add the mixers into the blender, how to clamp the lid down so the rubber gasket seals, and then lets him press the button marked liquefy, to hoots of shrill laughter, everyone barrelling around some invisible edge.

Coarse salt and bodies litter the fetid apartment the next morning. Stepping over her friends, into the sticky kitchen, I knock back a half-glass of warm, watery margarita. It is a first, but my throat opens easily as the sour pours in. The make-shift tip jar is empty, but for a few dull nickels glued to the glass, and Josh's little fingerprints smeared down the inside of the vase. Frozen concentrate limeade cans lie busted open on the counter, with butts stubbed out on the filmed, curling-up paper. The collective body of last night's party slumbers, and I slip out onto the fire escape, holding my breath and easing the window shut.

I feel it now. Not warm exactly, but warmer, and aroused by a sensation of newness flooding my body. I had held the liquid in my hand, then tipped it back, then swallowed. Simple.

Such medicine would always be on hand.

The fire escape floats, looming like a movie-set dolly, out into the dappled dust of the airshaft. Wrapping my fingers around the railing, I pan around at the neighbours' flower boxes and hanging laundry. Tulips and undershirts and men's socks, all in gray-scale, like a Hitchcock shot. I look across the shaft, into old Radcliffe Jean's kitchen window—her apartment packed with Nutter Butters and newspapers—giggle and wave at her silhouette, remembering how the last time we went to visit, she bent over in a sheer housecoat and Josh and I saw her big, dimply buttocks.

"I think it's gonna be a full moon," my brother announced, but Jean corrected him, saying she'd read in the Globe that it would be a crescent.

The sky seeps through brick, and shadows of clouds scuttle over cobblestone.

Some distant music rumbles, and I tilt my head; the subway sings, clear as revelation.

DEPARTURE

I was six-going-on-seven in the early fall of 1982 when Dad left Phoenix. Or Mom left, but Dad moved. These were secrets no one knew. Except God. (The man in the sky who watched to see if you were bad.) (He probably knew.) (Which was why it was important to smile, to be brave.) The man watched from the vast Arizona sky when I was a showy fraud in the second-grade talent show, wearing a matte-black leotard and pipe-cleaner whiskers, and mock-belting, "It's the eye of the tiger, it's the hmmmm of the fight! risin' up! to the challenge of our rival!"

There was no explanation for Dad's departure, just a careful dealing out of the facts as I watched his old VW Beetle in the driveway from the living room: we were going to stay with Mom for a while, Dad had to go work back east, either he or we would visit soon, and we would ride there in an airplane. Didn't I remember, Mom said, that I had been in one when we moved from Chicago? She loved this story: the one when I was just a baby, so beautiful that people everywhere stopped her to admire me, so small that she held me on her lap like a pocketbook and called the stewardess for help when I screamed during take-off. You couldn't believe the power of those little lungs, Mom said. And for such a quiet kid. The stewardess—thank god—had a trick and filled little Styrofoam coffee cups with boiling water, let the water sit for a minute, and then emptied them. With the cups still steaming, she hustled them back down the aisle to our row, where Mom clapped them over my ears. It held in the steam and sealed off the pain; that was the trick. I fell asleep on her chest—just like that—while Mom watched the plane's shadow trace along the southern edge of Lake Michigan.

CHANNELLING HARRIET THE SPY

I figured Dad's leaving had something to do with all those times Mom locked herself in the bathroom. Once inside, she would blow like a firecracker, and I would get the spins, the whole house twirling off into darkness. One night not long before he left and while watching *The Dukes of Hazzard*, Mom sat up as if struck by a thought and then dashed toward the bathroom. Dad rose calmly from his chair in the den and went over to the television and turned up the volume dial. "Go to your room," he said. "Mom's going to be okay." From my room, and with the pillow over my head, I heard only a muffled, under-water soundtrack: Mom hollering, Bo Duke hooting, and Dad begging Mom to open the door. From the crashing sounds, I pictured her like a cartoon dust devil of perfume bottles and bar soap and towels. I could never make out the words that mattered, could never translate the crashes and bangs into a story that made sense.

Years later, I heard a Robert Creeley poem in an under-graduate seminar and read the lines as if in a secret plea to Mom: "Love, if you love me,/ lie next to me./ Be for me, like rain,/ the getting out/ of the tiredness, the fatuous-ness, the semi-/ lust of intentional indifference./ Be wet/ with a decent happiness." From those early explosions, I learned only that Mom was fragile and Dad remote on the subject. Eventually, I solved the case of the explosions: they were "episodes," suicidal threats. Still, I thought if I could give her all my smiles and energy and cheer, that somehow Mom would get happy, that she would be drenched in it.

Toward the end of the year that Dad left, Mom, the baby, the dog, and I all moved up to a place in Moon Valley, then just a dusty outcrop of Phoenix proper with nubby hills and cactus scrub. Mom started night school, which meant Josh and I stayed late at the babysitter's, where we got to watch *Wheel of Fortune* and eat peanut butter sandwiches for dinner. Those sandwiches filled me with enormous relief and comfort, as did the game-show ditties. Mom took classes through the fall and winter, often pulling into the babysitter's driveway after dark. On those nights, her exhaustion was my ally—her Estée Lauder dialled down to a whisper. With the car purring quietly and the baby sleeping in the backseat, we rarely spoke on the rides home through the dark canyons that lay beyond the city lights. Instead of playing detective with Mom's mood, I might pump the window open and take furtive sips of the cool canyon air. I might scan for the jackrabbits that zigzagged through the darkness or sprinted across the road or dove through our high beams. Dad once said that they were just playing chicken with the car, that jackrabbits were too smart to get hurt. But that didn't explain why their tufty corpses littered the arroyos, or how some wet, alive panic lodged in my throat every time I saw one dash across the road. Like other wild things, they're drawn to light and sound, but once too close, they fall under a spell. But it's no game.

Jackrabbits jump in front of cars for no good reason.

ESCAPE ROUTES

Buddy, our tinsel-haired rag of a dog, was different after we moved to Moon Valley. He paced the entryway and played less. Mom said he was probably getting too old, but he wasn't too old to run away—always to the same place—seven miles back to the last house on North 36th. We kept a stack of missing dog fliers in the drawer of the entry table, but before we could circulate them, our old neighbours would usually call to say they'd found Buddy panting in the driveway.

Our new house sat on the edge of a desert preserve, and I began to retreat both into it and into an interior landscape, a place where I collected imagery, breath, and new words for the specimens of flora and fauna I found in the canyons. The geological terms fell short of my awe for the preternatural landscape. The desert was so much bigger than our little cul-de-sac, than us, than me. Its palpable indifference soothed me somehow—the cacti, red rocks, dust, rattlesnake peelings, and Lookout Mountain. This landscape stood aloof to my personal circumstances—and yet—it existed. It persisted even. Each morning I rose to find that the canyons were still there, performing their geological business.

Buddy never adjusted to our split family, nor to our move across town. At least once a week, he'd trot back to our old house in central Phoenix—or to at least as far as Bell Road, a six-lane boulevard, where I imagined him stranded on an island with other scraggly, lost souls. One day I left the door open too long as I watered the cacti out front, and Buddy tore off toward a construction site farther up the circle drive, and disappeared over a hill into the waterless canyons.

"Get in the car," Mom said and we climbed into the plushy beige of the family wagon. "You look right; I got left," she said, breathing in a great huff that lifted her bangs from her forehead.

"I ga back!" Josh called from his car seat. Panic thumped my chest, and I looked left, right, left, right—my little head on a swivel.

"Don't worry, we'll find him," Mom said. "He probably just ran back to the old house."

"Why Buddy confused, Mamma?" Josh asked

"He thinks we still live on our old street," Mom said.

"Is he looking for Daddy?"

"I don't know, honey, maybe."

"Are we gonna see Daddy?"

"Not today, hon; Daddy's in New Hampshire."

"Did Buddy go to Nampsherr?"

We made it over to Bell Road, then cruised through our old neighbourhood, winding in concentric circles around Black Canyon. I clenched the fliers in my chubby fingers, counted, and scanned for jackrabbits—for good measure. We searched for hours, each bend or turn or sign of movement bringing a rush of hope. Eventually, we grew hungry, silent, defeated, and Mom decided to head home. "Don't worry, honey." She patted my knee. "He'll turn up."

But somehow I knew that Buddy was gone forever.

PORTRAIT OF THE FAMILY BEFORE PHOTOSHOP

When I was teenager and after Mom moved to Boston, the three of us sat for her annual Christmas photograph on a brick patio located in the airshaft behind the brownstone she could barely afford on Beacon Hill. It was the same airshaft of my early woozy escapade and my own fantasy tableau, the same era. We wore matching black Jordache jeans and cream-coloured cable knit sweaters and posed with a glossy Golden Retriever. Except the dog wasn't ours—he belonged to one of the neighbours. Mom's lies always comprised lovely details: Golden Retrievers, brand names, schools from which she never graduated, and the names of towns that were never ours.

COMPOSITE SKETCH

I am my mother's daughter. My father's daughter. Not Daddy's Little Girl. Josh's older sister, forever, and to the moon. I favour my paternal aunts, with our fair, freckled skin, and our black-Irish eyes, the perfect little diamond of fight in them. Our oil-slick hair. I am New Hampshire and Massachusetts (and now Vermont), minus the scowl and accent. But I can drop my post-vocalic R's on a dime. And I will, if I think it might please you.

I am a creosotic whiff of Phoenix, where Josh was born. I am peelings of rattlesnakes and sunburns. If we're at a cocktail party and you present with flat vowels and the sibilant whine of the Midwest, then I was born in Chicago. In Mom's version her water breaks on the Elevated Train, but this is classic hyperbole. I gave her a belly kick. And it wasn't the EL—it was the commuter train out to Hinsdale.

Later, I am passing at the Boston Yacht Club in knock-off topsiders, holding my left hand up to the sun in an L-formation to remember port from starboard. P-O-R-T, four letters; L-E-F-T, four letters. I am a purple polyester accordion cheerleading skirt for the Catholic Youth Organization and estuary waders for the mud-flats at the Jackson Marine Laboratory at the University of New Hampshire. I am the cream-swipe of tawny lipstick and wood-smoked flannel and Doc Martens. I am San Francisco and Dr. Dre's Chronic 2001 album and skinny and handkerchief tops and one-night stands.

Later still, I am fat and Houston and Seven Jeans and

felony drunk driving and two months in the Harris County jail. I am the following orphaned chapter titles:

- Revelations of a Wet Brain in Stilettos
- Mirrors & Beer Goggles & Winged Eye Liner, Oh My!
- In Case of Emergency: Gin Recipes
- No Cocaine For Me, I'm Taking It Easy This Week
- Does My Hair Smell Like Fried Calamari?

I am Dad's disappointed face and Mom's helplessness and orange jailhouse scrubs and one good herringbone suit for the trial that I bought on sale at Macy's after stashing it in the juniors' department and asking Dad for a "loan."

I am all of the above, a mash-up. A composite sketch. I am Punky Brewster; no, Ally Sheedy; no, Neve Campbell; no, Tiffani Amber Thiessen; no, the Mom from Gilmore Girls. A passable Gyllenhaal. I am Velma from the Flintstone's, as my bunkie Yolanda declared with finality, while slammin' bones on the day room table and watching stories on the tiny jail television.

I am something else that finally gave, a barrel over the falls. In AA groups, I hear that I should be "grateful for the gutters," the consequences, the pain, and social facility. I should be grateful for these ranging experiences, but the truth is I am tired of fitting too many descriptions. Goodness requires too much, almost as much as the badness does not.

EARLY INSOMNIA

The winter I turned nine, we moved to New Hampshire to live with Dad in an apartment complex that smelled like cigarettes and burnt SpaghettiOs. Josh and I shared the one small bedroom, and Dad slept on an old couch in the living room. At six-foot-three, he dangled off of it from all sides, his spidery arms and legs draped over the armrests, his outside arm hanging limp on the floor like a vestigial limb. Dad would fall asleep with the television tuned into reruns of M*A*S*H or Hill Street Blues, the foil-muffed antennae crackling into the night. An early insomniac, I would rise in the dark and grab a snack or read, and hear his snores rumbling against the hiss of the television. I read during these long stretches of night, with a little flashlight I held under the covers. I read anything I could get my hands on—Judy Blume, the Ramona Quimby books, the Babysitters' Club series, an Amelia Earhart biography, *The Red Badge of Courage*, and even Dad's copy of *The Happy Hooker*.

Dad found me one night, the flashlight glow seeping through my polyester bedspread. He sat at the edge of the bed and scratched my back until I grew sleepy. "Use your nails, like Gram does," I said.

"Want me to crack an egg?" he asked. I nodded, then began to feel the happy tingle of yolk oozing down my scalp, my head getting heavy under Dad's hand.

WHITENESS IS A HELLUVA DRUG, 1993

Freshman year of college in New Jersey and moving into the dorms, Dad and I ride the elevator to the fourth floor of Mettler Hall. The third floor houses the Paul Robeson wing, named for the famed Rutgers alumnus and civil rights activist, and the elevator is crammed with Dad and me and four or five black upperclassmen. I suddenly feel conspicuously uncool (for coolness was perhaps the extent of my imagination of blackness then) as I clutch my tattered childhood teddy bear and pink shower caddy and notice that Dad's crew socks are yanked half-way up his pearly calves. Please don't mention New Hampshire, I plead mentally, looking over at Dad with his Tom Selleck moustache. I know I am white in the abstract, but for maybe the first time, I feel my own whiteness as a kind of contagion, a well-meaning malignance that rises in my body and soaks through me like warm piss. As the guys get off on the third floor, Dad and I wear twin idiotic grins, in case anyone looks back.

EXIT, ROUTE 95 NORTH, 1997

"I know you are reading this poem/ in a room where too much has happened to you to bear/ where the bedclothes lie in stagnant coils on the bed/ and the open valise speaks of flight." —from *An Atlas Of The Difficult World,* "XII (Dedications)," Adrienne Rich

The summer after college, faded like Polaroid emulsion. We furnished the cheap apartment with a bare mattress, a record player, boxes we meant to open, no television. Church Street, Asheville, North Carolina: prismed stained-glass, the pimp show on the street below, our first apartment, the question of spices. I waited tables down the street in a gingham smock, my nerves a-flutter, and my mind stuffed with pizza toppings and draft beers and feelings of dread for which there are only French and German words.

The mountains at dusk bent pink and green through our windows, and cheap lace curtains tangled in the breeze because I had to sleep with them open, I believed, so that I would not die. Droplets sizzled on asphalt and summer fumes rose to our windows like a wafting elixir. I dreamed of scabies and smoke and accidentally smothering the puppy that we adopted, also so that I would not die. I filled the apartment with superstition and breathing exercises and Puppy Chow. My childhood insomnia came back, and I filled the long night hours sitting by the open window and watching incense and cigarette smoke curl out into the void beyond the street lights.

I tried too hard that summer, buying towel sets and dragging chairs left for the trash up four flights in Southern heat, sponging out crumby cupboards with pine cleaner while listening to public radio and worrying about roaches, filling the cabinets with olive oil and vinegar, bags of sugar and flour, wondering how to compose a life.

How good you were to me, always holding my wet face, lifting the fire blanket of dread. Crouched in a field one weekend in the country, a screen door knocks in the distance, and your fingers hold fast in my armpits so I don't slip under. Your fingers on my wrist, saying yes, your pulse is fast. No, you are not dying. You ask the right questions, without irritating delicacy. You point out the hummingbird feeder; see, they eat sugar water out of that tube, you say, which helps, along with the juice held to my lips. But does not still the hyperventilation, the heartbeat drum, the words *I am going to die* this night, around this next bend.

I don't die, but then come the years of not living when I avoid airplanes, once hitching a bus from Jacksonville to Charlotte, when I dream only of plane crashes and drowning, when I try everything—hypnosis, belly breathing, and old-fashioned self-recrimination. When I avoid elevators but tolerate cars and count to 100 and back again on bridges and in tunnels. Agoraphobia, thanatophobia, claustrophobia, panic disorder, obsessive compulsive disorder, the books say. Medication, the doctors say, cognitive behavioural therapy, cardiovascular exercise, no caffeine! They don't say I will be okay. I think I might never.

You wanted to stay in the mountains after summer, kayaking the French Broad, and learning banjo, or selling Christmas trees in parking lots in Texas with other itinerants. But we left around midnight after I didn't show for work, lashing the mattress to the roof of the car with your water rescue rope, leaving behind the shower curtain, the pine cleaner, and a can of Raid; breaking our lease and defaulting on payment to Bell South. The puppy snored in my lap as you did all of the driving, down-shifting past the runaway truck ramps, and avoiding real and phantom hazards through the Blue Ridge Mountains. I read poetry, Adrienne Rich—*I know you are reading this poem*—the lines, a mental rope-tow, tugging me upright. *Because there is nothing left to / read / there where you have landed, stripped as you are.*

For whatever dubious reasons, I didn't begin to feel safe until Connecticut, until I knew, I suppose, that we were back in New England. After sleeping at a rest stop just outside of Hartford, the sun washed through the windshield and we got out to stretch.

CHERRY LANE, OGUNQUIT, MAINE

The puppy's eyes are milky full. We walk up the hill, imaginary heat from the lighthouse on our backs, and turn the corner onto Cherry Lane. Her paws soft on the snow, fur matting. Fat flakes wheeling into my face. We let her off the leash to run across the field into underbrush lined blue-white. Once inside, we flatten our sodden sweaters and hats on the floor next to the heater. Later that night I dream heavily of snow dissolving in salt water, the Atlantic blotting swell after another, torn riptide, undertow shorn.

LEAVING MAINE, 1999

Pine boughs wave in blurry smears across the windshield this morning. A boatman has come, taking me from you. The sky must be crying, the way my skin sags from the bone, the way my flesh litters the road and washes into the storm drains, along with fallen leaves and beach sand. I feel that I have to leave, but I don't want to anymore, and I am too young to understand that inertia and destiny are not the same thing. That falling in and out of love and back again is easy.

I etched everything into our old wooden bed frame, my tread, our rhythms, and bad poetry for you to find, like strands of my hair, after I'm gone:

> to be read by the heat of the moon
> when it is too late for sleep
> too much to stare down your blues
> in the steely backlight of the window glass.

I left you a map for steering in deep water. On nights when silked in melancholy or booze, we will wash up on different shores. But what if those moments become affirmations held through time? What if our minds and our memories are like maps?

All these years later, I like to think that parts of us stayed together, that on the morning I left Maine for good, our cells mingled in the storm drains on Cherry Lane, then washed into the Ogunquit River, where they met the tides and rode a rip current out into the Atlantic.

ONE-NIGHT STAND IN CHICAGO, 1999

With a sweet rinse of brine and fog and moonlight on Sea Point beach in Kittery, Maine, you removed my army and planted your sturdy bones in the honeycomb of my defences. Still, koan chatter rises from alternate waves. There are no miracles, I insist, as your reedy voice washes back to me in the early morning, as if out of a river in this stranger's bedroom wall that flows backward to the sky.

SAN FRANCISCO MUSE, 2002

I can't say why I had to stop and watch the rats on the sidewalk next to the gas station—who knows why—or why the bum we call Bird-Man spreads yellow grain on the asphalt, or why he rolls his shopping cart down Union Street, asking girls heavy with tit-jobs for money to feed his rare dove—he believes as much as the girls don't. He says that pigeons and doves come from the same family of birds. I want to believe too.

The man in #401 had a stroke we think. As I left for work the other afternoon, he limped off the elevator holding a torn grocery bag. Some fruit rolled around inside the cage and you put on a robe to help carry in his bags. A bottle of detergent leeched through the paper and the man and I smiled weakly. I had to rush to work and later you told me he reads poetry and talks to the radio all day, too loud. Who's to say what's too loud?

I'm tired of translating. The rats stuck somehow. After you walked ahead, I stayed and watched them for several minutes, darting from under the chain-link fence on Washington Street, out into the parking lot for the feed, then over the dumpsters in a scratchy conga-line behind the bar on Polk, their claws like hundreds of itty-bitty ice skate blades.

It's the same way first snows still catch me in the throat, the way I remember sitting on the counter pulling sips from a beer while you made me laugh for what seemed like forever.

SOLILOQUY, TIBURON FERRY, SAN FRANCISCO BAY, 2001

Every day I wake and walk to the corner for coffee and sugary scones. My body in San Francisco more leaden than Paris or Portsmouth. The way the light from another window lightens my step, the frame arbitrary. Windows in New Hampshire closed around white pines, around snow—and one in the hotel that I swung open while a Frenchman flushed the toilet and put on tight pants.

Dark clouds and tentative sunlight pooled over rooftops. I dangled a cigarette and some sweat over the ledge, the cool imprint of wrought iron on my arms, ashes dancing toward the Seine. Heading down the Rue de St. Sebastian (how the taxi driver chuckled when I read off the address as "Rue Street") toward the bar where every morning the dark, slim bartender fixes café au lait for me and Ellen. A skinny German Shepherd trotting down as far the Tabac, paws clicking staccato on cobblestone.

Angel Island could be a golden hulk of rock in Portofino or Cinque Terre. The names assigned usher a thousand breaths of meaning, words borrowed from Latin. I could have remained there, near the Bastille, drinking vin rouge from chilled milk bottles. My heart tied down to granite and the brown-green Atlantic. Suspended over San Francisco. *That* kind of ache. This inertial moment. This bay, that bridge, the blue, the rust, the chop, the white caps, that boat leaning into the horizon, its single white sail full as Dizzy's supple cheeks.

I can never remember the order of streets from mine to Broadway, whether Jackson comes before Pacific.

I can never forget that mallard-green sailboat called *Soliloquy* moored in Marblehead Harbor, or the absurdly-naked chicken sitting primly in a deli window in the Marais—or, that cheerful, red-faced clerk, waving from behind the display. The chicken was more like avant-garde taxidermy than food, propped as he was against the glass, feathers scattered beneath him. The whole tableau a metaphor for something wonderful.

THE PLATH TALKING, 2001

Rome was a twenty-four hour blur: the dusty Colosseum, Via Veneto, the Trevi fountain and a forgotten wish.

Instead of exploring the Vatican, I crossed my legs tightly in a police station, trying to staunch the image of their forced uncrossing in a smelly apartment a few nights before in Florence. Instead of slugging grappa with my friends and the too-celebratory old men in their row on the train to Rome, I sat on my own. I watched two women dressed all in black—probably mother and daughter—stow their luggage, then sit, and then hold hands. I put on my sunglasses and let my head fall upon the window.

I had not been to sleep, had been too tired to apply lipstick, and once the train lurched from the Santa Maria Novella station, and the cool glass kissed my cheek, I began to cry. I let fat tears roll down my face and neck and soak into my t-shirt like a bib. On the next day, I would take the same train back and file a report, but for this day, I would ride away through the flaxen countryside and wonder what to tell my father.

What is a good Catholic, anyway, I wanted to ask—a man who lies to get a girl back to his apartment? A woman who gets on the back of his scooter willingly?

Tell me, Daddy, something cool and camphor. Tell me that I am not a whore.

Que es un crimen, he said, in the Spanish we shared—how good I looked in red. Too good, he said.

I look so happy in the photograph at the Piazza Republica taken hours before, my tanned arm hooked around my girlfriend's tiny waist.

Too happy.

NOT-QUITE ONE-NIGHT STAND IN SAN FRANCISCO

Some months (or years?) after the rape, I am in a man's apartment in the Tenderloin in San Francisco. My first drug dealer was a petite white woman with blonde hair and fake tits who lived in the tony Marina District, but the deeper I get into my addiction, the less money I have and the less I stray from the front living room-cum-bedroom in the apartment, which I now share not with the boyfriend who moved out, but with a friend from the bar where I work. I have a dealer now who lives down the block, and who gives me a bulk discount on the cocaine I need to get out of bed. He is a soft-spoken black man, as big as a nightclub bouncer, maybe one hundred pounds more than my one hundred and thirty. He's nice and funny and the only person I am honest with these days. He racks some lines and we watch Six Feet Under and drink beer and eventually when it gets too late and I get too wonky to walk back home through the red light district, I lie back on the sofa. I can smell his musk and feel his body heat, and then we are spooning.

"I know you're not going to fuck me," he says. "And that's cool, I like just hanging with you." I exhale, relieved, and then feel as if I should, as an offering to his decency. His erection strains against the crook of my sacrum, but somehow I feel safe. He knows my history. "But let me tell you something," he says. "You are playing a very dangerous game."

"I know," I say.
"No, you don't."

And he was right. I didn't know what I was doing there. Aside from the drugs and the kind of company that required no pretence and no strings, what was I doing there in that moment, in his arms? I felt in my body a kind of power that had been lost, and I liked it. But this was not my own lost power; it was the power all white women have over black men, not that of attraction, but perhaps of history. Somewhere cellularly, or subconsciously, I understood this historical power. I understood our larger perceived roles: me, doe-eyed temptress, milky prize; him, dark, bestial danger. These were not roles I consciously believed, but they were there, lurking. I understand now that fluttering in my pelvis as a kind of nonsexual titillation. He was, of course, physically capable of crushing me, but the annihilation would be his.

POETIC JUSTICE

In the dream, he wears a cheap wolf costume and Chuck Taylors—the springy, piggy tail makes the whole thing hilarious someone says, but you tell them it's not funny.

In the dream, he writes from jail in flawless English. The envelope marked in heavy scrawl with one word that has no precise translation from Italian. In the dream you speak Italian and know the word but you note that it does not translate, as if to telegraph something to your waking self. From the envelope falls a photo of the man in a blue mechanic's jumpsuit, with your name in white embroidery like typewriter font on the lapel. Black hair and black eyes, dead marbles.

Then, flight, circling, ellipsis, flying low, you at the yoke, and the wolf-man towed behind in a prop. You buzz the Eiffel Tower and look back to see if the man seems scared.

Across an ocean, then skimming along shoreline ragged, in V-formation with a flock of Canada Geese. Your navigation is down, but you know it's the Atlantic coast because the sun slides down behind the far horizon—and a damp, salty air fills your nose. When you wake, you remember the pretty Serif letters, but not the word. All of the dreams are different, but in each the same swirl of Italian words. You wonder if dreams are just visually-interesting clichés (wolf-man? C'mon!) Just garbage jettisoned from the subconscious. But for one day at least you soar, and on the next night your dreams are blank.

VERMONT LETTER, 1998-2001

Wedding on a hillside. Before Italy. Everything now before and after. Friends gather in the green folds, buzz-saw hum of black flies. We sat up late the night before sipping wine from paper cups, citronella flaring into our lungs, butts swept from the barn. Your life, then mine. *Marriage is all about give and take*, someone's uncle slurs, his sweaty arm slung over one of your bridesmaids.

After Italy, I meet your plane, giddy as the time we built the fort, named the haven after our fathers. They said it was an *eyesore* and tore it down the next summer, along with my Sean Astin poster, while I was away at science camp. Ran next door and told you about the blond boy with a lisp who kissed me.

We had snuck out late, cabin's screen scratching our legs, then climbed to the top of an evergreen with limbs thick as waists. Up in the crow's nest, we caught our breath. The blond boy leaned in with his lisp. Love, I thought.

The camp pond below, shimmering. I didn't tell you about the slim canoe knocking against the dock like a heartbeat because we never know what stays. My heart, however muffled now, still beats in a blanket of summer moons I stashed deep in the barn cupboards the night of your wedding.

Here you are in San Francisco, and both of us hungry to go back somehow. Who am I to tell you to listen for the beat, to feel the swell of the current, to take it, to tack your line? Even as mine tugs east, and I turn against the wind.

Maps spread open on my kitchen table—showing you plot points and photos—from Paris to Amsterdam to Switzerland. At Italy we pause.

You left a marked-up map of San Francisco that crinkled from the damp that seeps from the Bay into my leaky studio apartment. Arrows to Stinson and Muir Woods, Alcatraz and the Wharf. All the places you wanted to see made me tired. I have seen too many places too fast.

The last night before you flew back to Vermont, you made out with a guy at some bar, while I did bumps with his baseball-capped friend in the bathroom. Tell me it's okay, you say, swiveling to me, your face flushed. You want me to tell you it doesn't matter. And it doesn't. But maybe not in the way we want it to.

I want to tell you that we'll get a rooftop apartment far away from everything, and we'll drink wine from paper cups every afternoon. That we'll be neighbours and best friends forever. I want to tell you I will come to the farm-house for New Year's. That we'll take wool sweaters and blankets into the barn and drink cheap champagne. I'll bring some good stories and we'll laugh clouds of frost. I'll fold snow into my pocket and wish I could stay.

SKYLINE, RAPT, 2004

This is the moment San Francisco ends. I climb up to the top of Russian Hill and look down upon the dark bay and North Beach, where the glinting lights and fog shroud Coit Tower and the Transamerica Pyramid. The therapist has said to practice breathing. Just try it. I am afraid to breathe deeply for fear of letting it all rush in. I look around to make sure no one is too close, but it's the middle of the night and few are out. So I breathe. I stand on the street corner at Lombard and Hyde, and I breathe in and out, like I am practicing Lamaze.

To be so excruciatingly alive is what hurts, the mystery of inertia, and the waiting around to get better. I think of a Seurat and the way you have to pull back to see the shape of the thing. I am a million dots of light and dark shaping, pulling back in surprise on my body, tight as a fist.

AN ALTERNATIVE OR SUPPLEMENTAL HISTORY

Here are the things you are/ were guilty of—guilt, that useless Catholic reflex you cannot unsee: You can't remember. Writers must, but you cannot. Whole sections of cities. The latter San Francisco years. Blots of Houston. Connecticut/ Rhode Island lives somewhere in here, but you can't remember, nope, not any of that ragged border-time. Where went Potrero Hill? You were there once in the psychiatrist's office peering out the window at your dollhouse city and praying for uppers. (2002 ish.)

The names of men you fucked. A (partial) list of those same men on the inside cover of the hardback evergreen Walden diary—poof. Packed in a defaulted storage unit, or maybe sold at the impromptu yard sale on Sutter Street when you left San Francisco for good. Your own naturalist history in a stranger's library, the names now (especially, you imagine, the Icelandic one with the umlaut) a curiosity, a passing anecdote.

Your first and last drinks, the bookends of your alcoholic life. You can't remember whether it was Kahlua at eleven and Jägermeister at thirty, or a Sombrero and Jägermeister, or a White Russian and not Jägermeister but something even more dreadful, in that final blackout. But you remember that you drank Jäger back then because it tasted medicinal and you liked to quip, "It's time for my medicine," to no one in particular. Back then, when you did everything in service of alcohol and cleverness.

Any linear timeline from oh-about-summer-fall-2000-to-2005. That RC Gorman print Dad gave you? You could remember only that the woman was faceless and Dad had kept a cheap poster version of the same in his office. He mentioned it at some point in the disappointed voice, but you couldn't remember the gesture, only that the painting was another metaphor you had somehow missed. The disappointed voice was in the same family as the we're-worried-about-you-sit-down voice.

Did they know you were snorting in the bathroom during breaks from the same sit down? Intervention wasn't a buzzword yet, but sitting you down said something. Sitting you down said you are not the daughter we expected you to be. You are not *A#1*. You are rotten and shitty; this is not what they said, but what you heard. What they said was you're too beautiful for all this. *All this* was code for the boozing and drugging and lying. *All this* was code for the San Francisco boyfriend nobody liked. *All this* covered many other sins no one wanted to say. And they didn't know the half of *all this*

You can't remember how you got lost, the details. How you got there, to that liminal no-place between the dead and the living. Off the map. From friends and family you were unreachable. You had to get lost to return. You can't remember the car accident and arrest. Only that you came back on the map at Interstate 610 and San Felipe in Houston. There you said find me.

***

And you still can't remember.

Even through and of the continuously sober years. 2006-

present. There are holes and fact-free smudges. And files collated in 3-ring binders that create a certain skeleton of what happened and who you were. You crawled across the floor of those years and places, and now you have these maps that feel vaguely familiar, like déjà-vu.

But you can remember certain medical and legal names, these names the buoys of those years (2005-2007), details that might rise to the surface in barroom trivia, but are otherwise useless. You can remember verbatim the words from the indictment for Intoxication Assault, the legal definition of Serious Bodily Injury, and that the punishment range for the offense is two to ten years in the penitentiary. That's the word the Texas statute uses, penitentiary, a place to be penitent, a place to repent.

You can remember that PAWS stands for Post-Acute Withdrawal Syndrome, but not how you felt in the early weeks after the crash. The family in the other car said you lacked remorse. Did you? You can steer around or through such black holes.

And who are those people on the edges? Some you remember, some you don't. Hands, but not names. Groping. Tracking the scent of these losses. Surely there were witnesses. You can make attempts to track them too. But they're not who you are after. You are after yourself. And what you can recover.

DRUNKALOGUE 1

I do not remember the first or last time I drank—appropriate bookends to this story. My first: either a Fuzzy Navel in my best friend's laundry room, or a White Russian in Dad's kitchen (Age fourteen?) Maybe my accounting is off and it was on one of the every-other weekends at Mom's city apartment. Dutiful eldest child, I would rise early after a romp for embattled divorcees and ponytailed man-boys—tiptoeing through a body count of slack jaws; collecting sticky glasses four-at-a-time, my hand like an electronic arcade claw; licking one finger gummed with salt and sour mix, and then the thirst. Perhaps just a nip while the adults slept off their hangovers. The variables are fickle, but the accounting compulsive, a futile effort to control the thing.

Dad and Stepmom kept a modest suburban liquor collection, assembled for a cul-de-sac block party and stored in a high cupboard over the oven. By the time I grew curious about its contents around junior high, the coffee liqueur was molasses, and the bottles were filmed with sticky fuzz, like fly paper.

Alcohol enclosed slowly. Indifferent to it throughout high school and college, I was busy with the good girl rat race—sports teams, honour societies, early admissions, and all-one-length chestnut locks, parted in the middle, and tucked behind my ears. At parties in the woods, I rarely drank, content instead with the occasional thrill of a boy's lizard tongue in my mouth, Led Zeppelin pulsing in my ears, or for a sudden swirl of flashlights and adrenaline, the town cops tracking us through an old cemetery as we streaked toward our parents' sedans and minivans.

I started drinking regularly when I moved to San Francisco a couple of years after college; then, a seismic shift took place. I still rarely thought about alcohol when it wasn't around, but when it was around (and it often was), it seemed like the elixir I didn't know I was missing.

I got a job as a cocktail waitress at a boutique hotel lounge, where I balanced a silver tray on my shoulder and click-clacked across the mosaic tile floors with a look-at-me swish of the hips. Glasses clinked and winked as if in a dishwashing detergent commercial, and gleaming bottles draped the back bar, a jewelled necklace of aquamarine, sapphire, diamond, emerald, and topaz. This movie version of life gave me the heady sense that I had finally arrived. I began to drink wine and neon-coloured "martinis" and to act out a posh facsimile of adulthood. I was twenty-something, smart, but not streetwise, and cute enough to be rewarded for naïveté. This was hope, yes, but also privilege. Unconsciousness is privilege.

I didn't belong in such a place, which was the delicious fraud of my emerging drunk-girl persona. While fucking advertising executives in the slick hotel rooms upstairs, I knew with the force of their blows that I didn't belong to this world, and it didn't belong to me. Still, these were the years when drinking was fun, when consequences revocable, and when I danced at bars and not on them.

Maybe the delicious fraud compelled me to repeated danger, or maybe fraud is the wrong way of looking at the thing, as a war of irreconcilable selves, split between good girl and bad, real and shadow. The drinking—a kind of permission I also didn't know I was missing.

More years followed when drinking *seemed* fun, if only because it was familiar. I noticed with peripheral awareness that my friends had since left the party of my permanent attendance. These friends moved on, into careers, and houses with nice backsplashes and intentional furnishings, while I stayed behind. I found new friends, temporary, in-the-moment types whom I met at bars or in bathroom stalls snorting lines off of toilet tanks. Or, I just moved. California, Texas, Connecticut. I hopped states like bar stools. *This place is a drag*, I would mutter, or *one horse town*, I'd slur, tottering from another. (Even in blackouts I was prone to cliché.)

BARTENDING JOKE, HOUSTON, TEXAS, 2005

At the end you drink, not because you want to, but because you don't know how not to. Almost-thirty, now under felony drunk driving indictment, and an underemployed bartender, you don't know what else to do—other than hang on—and the booze helps loosen the grasping.

Tending bar at a neighbourhood place in the Montrose in Houston, you keep a little notebook, as always, of characters, recipes, ephemera, to-dos, wishes, recriminations, overheard conversation. It's the one place where you tell the truth; it reveals, as Didion says, a consciousness on the outs with itself. It reveals a mind consumed with fear, a nattering of wires, a litany of sins.

"My life is a slow-speed chase," the cute alcoholic lawyer says to his gin and tonic. You look up from the notebook, stricken first, then excited. Yes, yes, yes, you think. You let your head back and laugh. You are flirting.

He smiles, surprised anyone was listening, surprised that a sad admission could tickle someone, surprised that someone in Houston appreciates irony. You look at each other with recognition. You have it too you want to tell him, knowing he'll be in a slurry blackout before long. You're taking slugs behind the bar, maintenance nips. "Me too!" you say. "Can I write that down?"

"Go ahead," he says, perking up, trying to think of another zinger. He looks sad, vaguely like a Basset Hound. You guess he's around your age, but seasoned like you, already a drunk, like you. Plenty of customers get sloppy here, but you can pick out the real drunks: their little regimens of napkins and straws, the specificity and sameness of their orders—it's always Beefeaters and tonic with a splash of Rose's lime, short, never, oh, I dunno, I feel like a mudslide today. You take the same medicine, the same way, at roughly the same time every day. Maybe they switch over to beer after a certain hour, liquor before beer in the clear, but there's a routine, a method, a drumbeat. They play the same songs on the juke, and repeat the same questions. Tell the same jokes. Go slack at the same hour every night.

This one is cute, and every time you tell him you are from New Hampshire, he says the same thing: "Oh, that's right. That's why you laugh at my jokes." And every time, you say the same thing back, "Only the funny ones." And maybe you wink or smile or toss your head.

Sometimes he'll grab your hands and ask you to marry him, and you will imagine it, the family oil money, the Southern charm, the jocularity, brunches with mimosas and country club dinners at holidays, and multiples of the same loafers. You are excited by the fantasy, and you go in the back and take a shot or a pull on your frozen margarita, which you drink whenever on the downstairs bar because the machine is partially hidden—half on the floor, half in the back, next to dry storage.

When you return, with a new bar rag or box of straws or limes or some other pretense, your cute lawyer husband is still sitting in the same place, his long legs bent into the creases of his khakis, but he's left you already.

DRUNKALOGUE 2

By the time of the arrest, you'd been thinking death for a long time. Maybe for years up until—timeline is fuzzy—dark thoughts and what the shrink called gestures. More low-grade stuff, proof it was in your head. Once, in San Francisco, Dad showed up in the emergency room. Early 20s. Is that what you wanted? For someone to come and take care of things?

You remember only bathtub, bandages, boyfriend on the phone, whispering in the hall, your crenulated hands moving like oars, water lapping at your knees. Was it your father on the other end of the phone or the ambulance? Was it the apartment on Washington or Sutter? Then the hospital and Dad leaning over the cot, and you sleepy. Were these bad dreams or your life?

By the arrest in Houston you're worse. Sometimes darkness snatches, sometimes it slips over you like a noose, or you drift under it like water. With the drinking it comes in drumbeats. Die. Die. Die. You want only to get gone. Oblivion is the X you drink toward. Drink. Die. At some point they become the same word. At some point you are not you. You are something else. Drunk animal.

Nights you drive fast, plunge for hours in holes where time and place is lost. You wake in some guy's apartment. You wake in some neighbourhood—the Heights, Montrose, somewhere off of Bellfort, or wherever. You think of Uncle Mike in the garage, waiting for the exhaust to take him. You have a premonition, but of something that already happened. The thing is entirely predictable:

56

you see that now. You barrelled to the edge and were returned to the world anyway, deposited in the parking lot of a Greek restaurant, doing the field sobriety dance. All the predictable moves. But what comes next surprises you, and you always loved a good surprise.

ENTROPY AS ISLANDS AS STARS, 2006

My version of exile on a desert island began at a rehab in Texas, stranded and left to face an inevitably cruel geography without chemical comfort. I could tell you about this island of years between a felony drunk driving arrest and two months in jail, or about the liminal interval of treatment where logic stole me before I lost nerve. But what could I say except that I had no defence left for drinking, no more drink tickets for the party, and so I went. I could tell you about that first month of sobriety—"thirty days and a hundred nights"—or about the two months thereafter when I attended my "ninety meetings in ninety days." I could catalogue the months during which sponsors, steps, and fellow recovering addicts and alcoholics saved my life, but my story isn't special. My island not an island at all, but rather, a strange constellation, a smear of shared pain and love. Somehow, I swam free, just as others have. I kicked the water and followed the person in front of me. I reached for the next wave.

Mom and I had come apart, set adrift to learn survival separately. Something about my getting sober had threatened our homeostasis, and when a rehab counsellor recommended separate family therapy—one with Mom and another with my father and brother, Mom got drunk, barricaded herself in a bathroom, and called a distant uncle who called my grandmother who called my brother. She was saying she would kill herself. Normally, my brother and I would drive over, coax her out, ply her with cigarettes, and soothe her with numbing words. But this time I had problems of my own. My brother wondered what we should do. "Nothing," I said. To save myself, I would have to leave her behind.

By the next February, the month of my felony trial, I had been sober a year, survived a road trip from Chicago to home in Houston with my new boyfriend's mom in a Mary Kay Cadillac, made new friends (sober friends!), and developed some new or long-buried healthy habits. I went to bed early, often with self-help literature that neither inspired self-hatred nor aroused my inner, carping debate club cynic. I read the literature without criticism and gave sincere thought to topics I would have scoffed at before: shame, boundaries, trauma, and inner children. I slept pretty well in those months despite my pink-as-a-newborn sobriety, the stress anvil that sat upon me, or the intrusive thoughts about what supplies I might need for life on the lam. (Money seemed to be chief among them, as wine steward, resume editor, or professional book report writer weren't viable career paths for my second life in a non-extradition outpost.)

Here, I also learned to nap and take walks and breathe. I learned that modest to-do lists were more easily accomplished than lists that began, "write great American novel," and ended, "overhaul psyche." I rode my bike to AA meetings and learned the network of secret bayou trails that spidered Houston's inner loop and connected most of downtown to my hubs in the Third Ward, medical centre, and beyond. Houston was a remarkably unfriendly city for bicyclists, and I was tired of poor road conditions, vanishing sidewalks, and the general indignity and terror of huffing on the thin edges of packed boulevards as shiny luxury sedans and SUVS sailed by just inches away. On the bayou paths, I worried less about visible crotch sweat or being out of shape or traumatic brain injury, and more about alcohol relapse, anxiety attacks, and two to ten years in the dreaded "penitentiary," a word worse than prison even, a place that conjured the worst *aegri somnia vana*: polio outbreaks, medical experiments, beatings, rapes, and soiled canvas straitjackets rigged with leather belts.

But the bike rides exorcised some of this flywheel hysteria, and I began to enjoy my commutes, particularly on Brays Bayou, which connected me easily to the rehab centre where I still attended meetings. I had to watch my heading on these paths because they were narrow with steep embankments down to the sleepy water's edge, but mostly I made mental drawings of aquatic creatures so I could Google them when I got home.

Brays teemed with huge, torpedo-like gar, catfish as big and brown as chocolate lab puppies, eels, paddlefish, sand sharks, and of course the gators and nutria that terrified me and almost sent me back on the roads. And though I was living with the constant pressing implacability of time, a bit like a character upon whom a piano might any moment come crashing out of the sky, and the ether felt heavy with consequence and choked with fear, I was also somehow okay. Remarkably okay. More okay than I had been in years. In exile, I had found higher ground.

And yet, entropy loomed. It would soon land: the piano, the hammer, the million little punches, the blade of the guillotine, the unmade bed, the roosting chickens, karma's bitch slap, the rock and the hard place, the bottom line, the crow, the humble pie, and a million other clichés that said things got bad and better at the same time. The myth which insisted that matter falling apart was not moving toward something larger, like islands or stars.

AFTERCARE

Just thirty-odd days out of treatment, I rode to a meeting with my new recovery buddy, Matt. He was a slow driver, perhaps extra cautious because of Post-Acute Withdrawal symptoms, and as he pulled his Civic past Hermann Park and down a block of shotguns in what seemed slow-motion, there, along the curb where storm water and flash floods sometimes ran fast, was—what the fuck was that? A scalp?

No skin was visible, just a fan of waxy black hair, like road kill, a discarded pelt, or maybe a fur stole. Though summer in Houston, I had seen some amazing shit in that city, shit that would stand your waxy fan of dead scalped hair on end. Of course we pulled over, and with that our friendship was sealed. There are two kinds of people in this world: those who drive past a possibly-human scalp lying in the road, and those who stop to investigate.

I had been under felony indictment by then for a year and a half. A chokehold of piss tests, county offices, courtrooms, AA halls, and panic attacks. Running ragged around my own mind with what-ifs and guilt speeches and innocence speeches and mercy speeches and apologies. Rehearsing apologies to the woman whose leg I broke in the crash became a drifting off ritual. Behind my fluttering eyelids she would reject me, my remorse would never translate, then the red light, the intersection, and nothing but the sweat I woke to some hours later. I could serve up to ten years in prison if convicted, and I often drifted from my AA literature to wonder about prison or to plot my way to the border. Never enough money in these scenarios, life on the lam seemed absurd, and a part of me wanted to stick around to find out what happened.

A few days earlier Matt had pulled over abruptly in front of the Children's Museum and pulled up the e-brake like an exclamation point. "Don't hug the sky puppet," the sign said, next to the three-story windsock man.

There are two kinds of people, and Matt and I are the second kind.

The scalp turned out to be a discarded weave, which made it somehow more comic, less grisly. We poked it with a stick, squealing, and clasping each other's hands. On the phone recently, Houston to Vermont ten years later, Matt and I reminisced about these early times when we held each other together. "Remember that weave over on Binz and Chenevert?" I asked.

"Yeah, what was the story with that?"

"No idea."

"I wish I knew," Matt said. "Me too," I said, "me too."

NOT A PLACE ON ANY MAP

Phoenix to Yorba Linda, 1982

Mom hauls west on I-10 through mirage and heat shimmer, but there is no time for physics because she wants to make it to Blythe by noon. She is leaving my father, or he is leaving her, and getting out of Arizona by morning seems important. She banks miles for hours, and I track the inches with my thumb-joint on the map. The baby waves his fat limbs from the car seat and babbles, while I turn knobs on the Etch-a-Sketch, drawing the last Phoenix house before I forget what it looks like. Absorbed in perfecting the arch over the doorway and shading the suitcases on the front step, I look up occasionally to see Mom lighting slim cigarettes and tapping on the steering wheel. The air grows cooler near the Colorado River, and Mom pumps the window open and reaches her arm out to tilt the side mirror. Toto comes on the radio, and the baby bounces as Mom cranks the dial. The song is "Africa," and the car is awash in the crash of cymbals, and synthesizers, and a feeling that everything could be okay in the next place. As a rule, Mom sings the wrong words: "God bless the rays down on Africa." All these years later, I still sing the wrong words too, part muscle memory, part homage.

San Francisco to East Coast, 2003

On our way out of California in a Civic packed to the headrests, my friend and I turn off Interstate 10 in Blythe, the last stop in California, 607 miles southeast of San Francisco and 150 due west of Phoenix. I'm leaving behind cocaine and some bad years and now that I'm in Blythe, the memories reach for me. With decent reception, I extend the little black antenna and call Dad on my new mobile phone. "I just wanted you to know we've made it to Blythe," I say. It sounds like the words the father might repeat on a Dateline special, after some terrible accident, after his daughter has been left in pieces for the desert coyotes. "She just wanted to let me know she'd made it to Blythe," the father might say ruefully, searching for some meaning in a last phone call.

"Ah, Blythe," Dad says, acknowledging a place we often stopped on our way to visit family in Yorba Linda. "Halfway between Phoenix and L.A." Blythe is remote, has no fraught history, offers only milkshakes and gas. This is how we share affection, by trading panned nuggets of trivia that intersect with shared places, like how Richard Nixon was from Yorba Linda, or that Houston, Texas is the fourth largest city in the United States. We talk in map points and routes and population density and flora and fauna. I tell him about the coyotes and arroyos and jackrabbits and how they pull from me a deep nostalgia for the desert I didn't know was left, from the early child-hood years before we moved back east. I don't tell him about the sadness that swamps me, how it feels new and familiar both, or how I wonder if Blythe is a place to let it in finally, a place with no past, a place where someone could go to disappear.

Florence, Italy, 2001

I am 6,097 miles from my apartment on Russian Hill in San Francisco, in a cold, stone office in the bowels of the stazione policia, on Via Zara in Florence. The night before, I had dinner with friends on the Piazza Della Repubblica, fifteen minutes by foot from the police station. The night before, I wore an outfit I bought special for the trip: red pedal pushers and red blouse, heeled sandals, and lavender head scarf.

We chatted gaily with our waiter, who joined us after his shift for Fernet Branca and Prosecco. He spoke little English, and I little Italian, but in broken Spanish and flirty eye contact, we managed well enough. My friends and I and the waiter walked over the Ponte Vecchio, but at some point while browsing the trinket shops and smoking cigarettes with our arms draped through the stone portholes over the Arno, he and I drifted from the group. At another point, I figured they'd gone back to our hotel, and he offered a *"corto trayecto"* on his moped. Still drunk, sun-baked from the day, and dizzy from the ridges of terracotta rooflines undulating by, the ride exhilarated me in those first moments. But after twisting down more dusty lanes and bumping over cobblestones and emerging onto a faster, wider boulevard, my giddiness evaporated. I began to feel sick and to spin, adrift from my friends and the hotel and the center of town. He slowed the moped to a stop, hopped it onto a sidewalk in front of an apartment building and with his strange, sweaty hand, the nice waiter led me up a flight of steps and into a small apartment.

Why did I go? I think now, as a translator from the American Consulate mouths the Italian words for the images that flash into my mind without a linear timeline. The words sound cheerful when the nice lady says them in Italian, the words for *oral sex*, for *finger penetration*, for *erect penis*, for *without consent*, for *kick-start scooter*, for *champagne headache*, for *swarthy waiter*, for *slim build*, for a *Calabrian driver's license*, for *his email address scrawled on a napkin*, for *No*, for a *partial apology in Spanish*, for a *cigarette afterward*, for a *walk over the only bridge in Florence to survive World War II*, for *permission to call my father*, for *the correct change in Liras*.

High on adrenaline and instinct and a lifelong good sense of direction, I lead the officers back to the man's apartment, some four-plus back-switching miles from the piazza. Since I have the napkin with his name and email address, the officers match it with one of the occupants listed in their records. "*Ben Fatto!*" one of the officers shouts and pumps his fist from the front seat of the little police car. "It means good job," the translator says. "I know," I say. When I pack for my flight just hours later, I flatten the words on the police report in the bottom of my suitcase like a freighted souvenir, underneath the red pants and blouse and stacked heels I wore the night before. I realize then that my panties are gone, probably still in the man's apartment. Once on the plane and headed back to California, my seatmate asks if I'm going home, and I nod, then: "Well, yes, I live there," I say, thinking home is not a word I understand anymore, not a place on any map.

1900 West Loop S Service Road, Houston, 2005

This is the address in tidy block print on my arrest report for drunk driving. Google Maps converts that same address to 1900 W Loop S Fwy, Houston, Texas, 77027. The crash occurred, technically speaking, on the frontage road, a feeder to the freeway proper. The 610 Loop is the major artery that encircles the city in a blobby square. Those who live "outside the loop" are considered suburbanites, and those who live "inside the loop" urbanites, though the population density feels mostly the same in Southeast Texas, where land is not a premium.

The loop confuses me, because its name changes depending on the direction travelled, and the shift from one arm to the next—while clear on the map—isn't all that clear on the ground. Houston is not a city of landmarks—no ocean on the left if headed north as in San Francisco; no ocean on the right if headed the same direction on the East Coast. No arroyos or piazzas or characteristic predatory fauna, as in other places on other maps. Just mile upon mile of new construction, bleached-out faux-Mediterranean shopping plazas, ice houses, apartment complexes, and then more miles of pavement, shiny SUVs, and chain restaurants—all the way to the haze-smudged horizon line.

Starting at the accident and arrest site, where the freeway crosses San Felipe, and following it all the way around the city, the loop runs thirty-eight miles, comprising the West Loop South Freeway, the South Loop West Freeway, the South Loop East Freeway, the East Loop Freeway, the North Loop East Freeway, the North Loop West Freeway, and the West Loop North Freeway. Though clear in a technical sense, the sameness of the Houston landscape, along with these names, only disorients me further.

Early after the crash, I look up the location on Google compulsively, travel down a rabbit hole of memory and geography. I map the site to my apartment, to my job, and inevitably to other places. I shuffle my memory and pull places like cards.

The compulsion helps me play chicken with time and reality and trauma. I know this now. But then I'm thinking only that if I can pinpoint the location, I can somehow reshuffle the deck and change my hand: the Jeep un-crumples, popping into perfect relief, then reverses out of the crash and back down the feeder road. I pour wine back into the bottle. I wonder about certain ifs. If I had left work earlier or later. If I had not been drunk that night. (But on what night was I not drunk? I couldn't remember.) If I had not moved to Houston. If it had been raining. If. If. If.

From the accident site, my apartment at 1901 Binz is 8.7 miles. I had covered less than a mile from where I started in Uptown Park, so I probably wouldn't have made it home anyway, presuming I was headed there.

***

When I look at maps of where the accident occurred all these years later, I am drawn to its proximity to I-10, a possible escape hatch to other places far from my problems and even to places from my childhood. What if I had gone the other way, north to I-10; would I have made it, spared everyone? I realize it's a kind of magical thinking, but I look at the map and the 3.1 miles to the Interstate and I think drive, girl, drive west—back to Phoenix or Blythe, to a place before Florence and San Francisco and Houston, to a place before your own high mileage.

I-10 runs 2,460.34 miles from Florida to California and is the southernmost transcontinental highway in the Interstate Highway System of the United States. Driving west on Interstate 10, you can put a lot of distance between yourself and a place you shouldn't be.

GETTING OUT—1201 BAKER STREET JAIL, 4C1, HOUSTON, TX, 2007

I was released from jail on an Easter Sunday at 2AM by way of a downtown Houston loading dock. The thirty or so other inmates and I were deposited onto that loading dock at a witching hour and left there, put out like trash, shivering humps of nothing, just trying to make our way home. Snow fell ethereally on the streets, which made the city seem beautiful as if transformed by the sleight of a magic trick. For that moment, the snow also made her seem like home. It almost never snowed in Houston, Texas, much less in mid-April on an Easter Sunday. That is was snowing, that it was Easter, that I was going "home" to my apartment only a few miles south of the jail, and that I was now closer to my final escape from Houston; these were just facts. But if facts could be beautiful, these were. If facts could be stars of snow that poured out of the impassably gray sky like tiny chains of paper dolls and made your face wet both from their anointment and the joy of their coldness and wildness, then these were those sorts of facts.

GETTING OUT—1201 BAKER STREET TO 1901 BINZ, VIA FANNIN, 3.9 MILES

Unlike many other inmates deposited into the eerie pre-dawn wasteland of the country's fourth largest city, I had people waiting for me with a warm coat, a warm car, and cigarettes. Most of my fellow released inmates were black, brown, or what was called "hillbilly white" in jail. My brother saw me first, before I saw him, and he grabbed my arms and we did a kind of giddy, standing-in-place dance and exchanged a flurry of words and hugs. I saw Keith then, my love, the man who had stayed through, first the back of his leather bomber jacket and how it gathered at his narrow hips, and then as he turned to face me, I ran to him, put my face in his coat and reached up to put my arms around his shoulders. Was he always so tall? His face was smooth on mine, and I knew he had shaved for the occasion.

I wish I could say I was kind to those other women then, that my ministry of justice began immediately, but the truth is that I wanted to get the fuck out of there, to blaze beyond that block and beyond the other downtown Houston blocks I associated with "the law." In my mind, the short miles from here to home represented a gauntlet we had to run from peril to safety.

The truth is my brother was kind—offering transportation suggestions and cigarettes out the window of our idling car to a couple of women who had gathered around.

No. No. No. Whatever it is, no. This was the refrain that ran through my head as Keith opened the door for me to climb into the back seat. I was absurdly dressed in my court clothes from sixty-one days earlier—a pink cashmere sweater with a pearly silk collar, plaid culottes, black sling-back heels, and Keith's bomber jacket. I was sure they wanted a ride somewhere—deep into the Third Ward or the Fifth Ward or to Sunnyside—and I was wary of giving them one, didn't trust them, didn't trust the cops, and didn't trust that this brand new freedom was real. The Fifth Ward was just too far away and Sunnyside was out of the question.

I considered taking them if the request was for the Third Ward, as we lived there, right on its beginning-to-be gentrified edges. I liked to call my little section of the ward, which was being rebranded "the museum district" by white real estate builders, not the hood-hood but the hood lite. It was a historic and historically black neighbour-hood with a block-by-block mix of stately brick houses, Art Deco fourplexes, ramshackle shot-gun houses, and catfish shacks, a neighbourhood plagued by an "increased police presence," where the street drugs emerged on the streets and not on the slick glass table-tops of McMan-sions as over in River Oaks or Memorial Drive. There would be police patrolling the area, as usual, and three white people going by in a little hatchback would only raise eyebrows if we were speeding or driving erratically. But the addition of these two black girls, who seemed to be waving yet another person over, could spell prob-lems, and I didn't want any more problems. Not tonight. Somehow their very presence in our car would take us all back to jail. We hadn't even left jail, not really, but I felt that if we didn't get out of there fast, I was sure to go back.

I made a cutting motion across my neck to my brother as we made eye contact in the rear view mirror, and I rolled my window down.

"I'm sorry," I said to the women. "But we gotta go." The taller one who was from my pod leaned in for the dap she taught me how to do after her all-black-team had recruited me for volleyball one day after seeing me serve.

"Don't go teaching all your white friends your new moves," she said.

I laughed. "I won't."

"It's cool," she said. "I know you'll be good, teach."

Teach was a nickname I had earned on the pod for helping some of the other girls with letters to judges or translating legalese or crossword clues. I wasn't a teacher yet, but I would be in my next life, and they saw it before I did.

RELEASE, WIMBERLEY, TEXAS

Somewhere over the course of the following weekend at a cabin Keith had rented in the Hill Country, I began to feel a little better, not relieved exactly, but like I would be returned to life—not to my old life, for there would be now and always a distinct before and after—but to my new life, perhaps even my real life.

It happened by degrees, while playing the old Genus Edition of Trivial Pursuit on our rented veranda with my wooden sandals tapping the flagstones as I fretted over my answers, and later again, while sitting with Keith, holding hands and watching smoke curl around his dim figure in the pink wan of dusk, smoke filtering through the ranch fences and live oaks. I felt a little better still as we stopped road side on our way back to Houston at a cardboard sign announcing a puppy sale. There was a corral of them, in a makeshift pen of chicken wire, a writhing, soft mass of grey, black, and white Australian shepherds. Of course I wanted one, wanted to scoop one into my t-shirt and hold him to my face, but it was enough just to feel his soft fur, his warm, gritty tongue on my palm, and his sharp teeth like cacti in my fingers.

It was enough to be just a little less afraid upon returning to our apartment, where we would spend another four months saving money, planning, and working out our exit. It was inevitable that we would leave Houston, and that we would put the whole ordeal behind us in a strict physical sense, though I knew the experience would be forever with me and in me, in some important place.

***

On our way out of town, we stopped at 1200 Baker Street—my address for "60 days and a wake-up." Dawn still and under the streetlights, the building looked unfamiliar, but then, I had seen it only once from the outside. We parked at the corner of Baker and Top next to a lot packed with Harris County Sheriff's Department transport busses. I wanted to stop for a photo, but also because I needed to see the jail, to nod at it and punctuate the end. Keith took a photo of me not-exactly smirking underneath the street sign of the 1200 block. As we stood there, some cops climbed up the steps and went in, and others came out. A street sweeper ran parallel down San Jacinto Street. We lingered for a minute, and I had that feeling that I should say something, but I didn't.

It was early still, and I felt road-punchy already: my thoughts turned to coffee, maps, and folk tunes—to the little adventure before us and the big one after. For some moments I imagined that I could bottle and save the feeling I had as I watched the Harris County Jail disappear from view. First, the street entrance façade disappeared as we turned right off of San Jacinto, but then the edifice reappeared intermittently between the buildings like the glow of a moon behind scudding clouds, and then again as we got on I-10, where for a few last moments, we had a short, running view of the courthouse and the whole block.

I knew to leave the place was to leave some of the experience behind. I would have to give the feeling back to the world; I couldn't keep it. We could drive east now, past the city lights and limits, and through other places beyond Houston's shadow, to someplace that we might call home.

COURAGE

The high jump, like so much else, is just physics: $U2 = 2gH$, the formula for energy, acceleration, and height, explains how Dick Fosbury took the gold in Mexico City in 1968 with his unusual backward sail over the bar. The announcers dubbed his signature move the Fosbury Flop, but I don't see any flop. I don't see any physics either, only magic.

Even in Vermont, with more than ten years of sobriety and relative stability, I am still afraid to flop. Again and again, I skirt this familiar conscious edge with my mind's cartoonish miasma at my back—all of its limitations and lost points and monkeys and awful fucking chatter. Still, being here, then going there or anywhere or beyond is the point—the singular, impossible point. And sometimes the going is also the reward. The point is to inhale from deep within, to hold your breath, and then to throw your whole body into fear's dark maw. The point is to leap because others have done it before, and their doing it mattered.

The math is simple: the lower one's centre of gravity, the less energy the jumper uses to clear the bar. But math can't explain the magic. I want to know how the jumper steels herself as she trots the twenty meters in toward the jump. I want to know what she whispers to herself just before leaping.

THE GEOGRAPHY OF HAPPINESS, RANDOLPH, VERMONT, 2012

I want to sit with coffee, but the dogs press their noses into my legs and dance around me like a maypole. Teeth unbrushed and slimy, no bra, salt crystals in my tear ducts, *ah hell*, and I shoulder into my coat, hook up my babies, and shoo them through the doorway. *I can't live here forever,* I think, rounding the corner and onto the little stone bridge that passes over the Third Branch of the White River. *Too white, too smothering.* A polite way to think I am bigger than this place.

A larger self like a balloon tethered to and floating above the whiny one suggests I acknowledge that I am my own problem—restless, unsatisfied, wherever I go there I am. And each time I am forced to learn this—San Francisco, Houston, Asheville, now here—it is like revelation, so I'm not as smart as I think.

We cross the bridge and the laundr-o-mat parking lot, where a woman wearing spandex and fitness bands high on her fat arms hides behind a crossover-SUV with her two blonde labs, past the handsome cultural centre, the library cast in Greek Revival; *see, this is a nice place,* the balloon head coos, and I start to come around to her way.

I cast my line into town and look around for little tugs, nibbles of insight. The multi-congregational red brick church that "saves" town drunks and addicts pulls me first toward the sandwich board propped out front, the board that offends and tantalizes with its Bazooka-Joe brimstone wisdom. I always admire it for its pithy fear-mongering

76

and cobbling of old and new. Today the sign reads, "A Lifeboat Does No Good If the Drowning Man Does Not Climb In."

Looking down, I see the crab apples dot the sidewalk with their smashed-wax husks, and among them a dancing chain of dewy paw prints—bigger ones for the Boxer, and smaller ones—like imprints of baby feet—for our Pit Bull mutt. Then something that rarely happens, they both arch over their hind legs at the same time, dumping onto the church lawn with lovely symmetry. *Bravo*, I think as I bend down with my grocery bag.

It's not until crossing back over the stone bridge when I notice how far the river has shifted its course; the backhoes flatten a beach that was just a spit a few weeks ago before Tropical Storm Irene. The riverbed is changed too—streaked with muddy lines like great claw marks, and I remember the force of the water that day, like a train roaring through town.

We watched it from our third floor dining room, as it toppled its banks, marching forward, as it swelled over Prince Street and into the fields of Queen Anne's Lace behind our shed, and all the way down Park Street where the ball fields were sponges, and then past the fields into the little trailer park where people watched the horror of selection: rolled up carpets, lawn mowers, oil tanks, decks and railings, old card tables, and hanging plants—plucked like fruit into the water, along with some of their houses. "Marriage is a discipline," I remember a friend telling me, and I think, *Life is. There's a discipline to tuning in and to liking my own life*, I think as I remember your hard, hungry mouth on me last night, and I am wet with a decent happiness.

GETTING OUT—BEYOND TEXAS

I wonder now if I touched the other inmates' lives in the way they touched mine. I wonder how I will ever repay them, the women who gave me the gift of my other education, perhaps even my real education. For months after I got out, I was jumpy and afraid of landing back in jail. I was obsessed with jail itself. Suffering from PTSD, I talked about my experiences all the time, and friends and family wisely encouraged me to move on, live my life, to put it all behind me.

Though I have lived my life in the ensuing years, I can't say that I've moved on, and I can't say that I want to. In Toni Morrison's novel, *The Bluest Eye*, Pecola says, "Anger is better. There is a sense of being in anger. A reality and presence. An awareness of worth." Harris County may have released my body, but a part of me will remain there, close to the anger, and closer still to my mislaid sisters.

ALLEGORY, AMERICA, 2015

She is unconscious, few vitals, gone through godly membrane. Passed, we say, politely. But what if she is not all the way gone? What if she is suspended only, in arrest? Perhaps a flash of heat, electricity, or plunge into ice bath. Perhaps she is only sleeping—stale, nostalgic dreams. Fear slumped into habit, and she went off every day—left dreams on the bedside, in drawers—took lunch and inventory. A good day is productive, hauls an objective yield—of fish, of numbers, or meetings from which people leave feeling smug. She went off to tend to another's weak vision, and yet with her own stake, acres on which to collect thermoses and tote bags and to-do lists—a place at which to share the collective delusion that any of it matters. Or, that any of it matters in the right way. This is not the vision worshipped in schools. Here, people are not nimble and principled, but sallow, satisfied, driven by fear or comfort. The weak army of the smiling and effective ascends, soars even. She let the dreams at home collect pollen and skin cells and hideous mites. She failed her history classes, on the wars and ravages; she slipped the noose of the lessons of the lynchings. The colossal weight excised from the textbooks, her conscience mute. And though ruddy and plump, a malignancy has stolen her. No more rock and roll roiling her pulse.

Only endless wars and work and foodstuffs and consumptive inertia. She is America, an autoimmune disease, an ouroboros, the worst sort of recidivist. The tragedy was falling asleep at the helm of disaster. The tragedy was sailing headlong at myth. The tragedy was slowing her pulse and letting her body drift toward Florida, Ferguson,

Baltimore, and every other post-racial mirage. No matter that the vessel wasn't sound to begin with, she should have steered it better. But she is on the iceberg now, swirling search lights over the gridlocked government and the slain in the noon streets and the white hands caked with gunpowder and the pale indoctrination in the schools. The ship is listing still, but starlit and woke, at last. And those light pulses are not stars: they are the sky on fire.

ELIXIR WASHES ASHORE, 2016

"It was reported her hat and cane had been found on the bank of the Ouse River. Mrs. Woolf had been ill for some time." –*Virginia Woolf Believed Dead*, by special cable to *The New York Times*, April 2nd, 1941

A year since we bought the house along the river and weeks since it rained. But now, thunderstorms crackle the edges of sky, perhaps in the next valley, or in the one over from that. Close enough that standing on the back deck, I feel a whisper of wetness on my arms, like the spray from a prow after a lone wave, a sensation I wait for again and again. The dogs tap around the house, circling one corner and sitting, then getting up again to perform the same ritual in another corner. Are they looking for safety or comfort, or simply driven to complete the dance? The storm cracks a whip over the house, and Jazzy, the rescue Pit Bull with bad nerves like her human mamma, dashes—as if under a hail of enemy fire—from her pallet to the bathtub. Diving into the tub, the shower curtain crashes down upon her, and there's nothing to do now but go to the medicine cabinet for the doggy sedatives. The storm is coming.

The river is as low as we've seen it, the riverbed a bleached boneyard of granite and glacial till, and I am—as usual—antsy for the rain, for a deluge, for something to happen. I scramble along the riverside, picking trash out from between rocks and gnarled knots of the boxelder roots that cling to the riverbanks, exposed by erosion. *But I shan't go mad*, not today, I think, as Keith grins from the yard. He hitches one pant leg up, leans on the weed eater like a cane, and waves. "No hat or cane," I shout, but he

81

cups one hand over his left ear to indicate he doesn't hear. I've been reading Woolf and thinking about suicide—not as something I want to do, nor as a romantic gesture—but as an act that is both single and cumulative. It's one act in a long line of others, like fetching the mail, making love, and baking pies, but it's one that wins out somehow. I imagine Woolf filling her pockets with these heavy Vermont stones and then drifting down river. I imagine her sitting lower and lower in the water, until she spins out of view, around the bend in the river by the dairy farm. But I allow that drowning oneself in such shallow water would be difficult, if not comically macabre.

I yank a mud-caked skein of pantyhose free from the box elders and hold them up for Keith's appraisal. "Creepy," he yells. As usual, I'm looking for something: an image, an object, something of use, a release. I find one feedbag, one can of Skoal, an ear of corn (munched clean), and a small, flat bottle of something called "Dr. True's Elixir, Established 1851, Auburn, ME." Later, I look it up online and find it was an herbal remedy for pin worms, something akin to bitters, along with wild claims of digestive rapture and testimonials detailing expulsions of spotted lizards and live, eighty-foot tape worms. Medical researchers later debunked the claims, and Dr. True had to remove all mention of worms from his advertising, yet sales of the remedy continued to skyrocket. I suppose everyone wants to believe in an elixir.

I bag my trash haul and put the elixir in my pocket, but I am still waiting for something. The storm. We need the rain, yes, but more than the rain, I need the relief that comes after the rain, the relief that comes after the awful black mounting and the storms marching upon the land. I need the rain to come and wash me clean.

BAGGAGE CLAIM

I bought the suitcase in a train station in Milan, just before Florence, and before everything that came after. When I cut my trip short, the suitcase held all of the items that had been in the man's apartment, plus all of the items from the trip that would forever trail to all of the things that changed me in that apartment—to a permanent disembodiment. The arrest report that never went anywhere, "what I was wearing"... I bought it in a pinch when my backpack started to unravel, and since the suitcase cost a small fortune in ill-prepared tourist tax, I've kept it now for fifteen years. I brought it with me when I moved from west coast to east, then to Texas, then back east again. It's just a bag, I've always told myself. I'm nothing if not practical, and it still works okay. But it weighs a ton, it takes up too much space, the wheels are wonky, and of course, it's not just a bag. There are new, lighter models with twirly wheels and no memories. So this morning, I rolled it out to the end of our driveway and left it next to the road. I marked it FREE because it's already cost so much. If I had known how good it would feel to put old luggage out on the curb, I would have done it years ago. But some learning is slow. If there's something you need to let go of, throw away, or put out for someone else, I hope you can. Holding onto it is harder.

LETTER TO ALL THE PLACES

On gray, wintery nights like these I will walk longer with the dog, my gait slower. Maybe we'll go farther down Main Street and turn right down Church. Jazzy will sniff and wag and pee and then kick wet leaves and ice flecks back over her spot. Then we'll double back. I'll be listening to my ear buds, to rebel and folk and fight songs, climbing into some sweet melody of melancholy. On such nights, thinking about everything and nothing, I will cry out into the night—sending some urgency into the world.

On these nights or on others, I will wake up in the middle of the night and go down barefoot, sticky-step into the kitchen and open the fridge. I am looking for orange juice and for the pour of light that breaks into sadness. It's four or six or eight or ten years later, and I don't pray like I used to when I first got sober. I don't keep my shoes under the bed, don't say help me in the morning or thank you at night, but sometimes in the middle of the night, I will drink some juice and then fall onto the floor of the little dining room, the moonlight silver and slivering into the turret, my favourite room. I will put my head on the window sill next to the cool glass and I will weep.

Am I thinking of Yolanda? Or the other inmates? Am I thinking of so many women waiting to be believed? Am I thinking of the friends who saw me through early recovery and jail? Am I thinking of my fractured family? Or my own fatique? Or the sparks that lit in the classroom that week? Am I thinking help, thank you, please, bless those who have not?

Whatever I am thinking is a kind of prayer.

ACKNOWLEDGEMENTS

Some of these essays, in some form or another, first appeared in other publications.

"An Autobiography of Arrivals" was originally published as "Arrivals: An Autobiography" in *Pithead Chapel* (November 2013).

"Departures," "Escape Routes," "Portrait of the Family Before Photoshop," and "Channeling Harriet the Spy" appeared in the longer essay, "A Decent Happiness," which was published in *Pithead Chapel* (March 2013).

"Early Insomnia" was first published on *Brevity*, in the longer essay, "Stay Awhile with Your Own Ones: A Father's Day Essay" (June 2014).

A version of "Skyline, Rapt," originally appeared in *Fourteen Hills* (Fall/ Winter 2001).

"An Alternative or Supplemental History," appeared first on *Rawboned* (January 2015).

"Drunkalogue 1" and "Drunkalogue 2" were published together as "Drunkalogue Diptych" in *The Pinch* (Fall 2015). Portions of "Drunkalogue 1" also appeared in the longer essay, "The Right to Remain," which was published in *The Rumpus* in 2015 and named a notable in Best American Essays in 2016.

"Entropy as Islands as Stars," was originally published in *New Madrid Journal* (Winter 2016).

"Not a Place on Any Map," originally appeared in *New Mexico Review* (Spring 2015).

"Getting Out—1201 Baker Street Jail, 4C1, Houston, TX, 2007" appeared first in the longer essay, "Life After Jail," in *Seven Days* (August 2008).

"The Geography of Happiness" appeared in the longer essay, "The Geography of Consolation," which won the New Millennium Writings Nonfiction Prize in 2013, and was subsequently published in the *New Millennium Writings* 2014 anthology.

"Allegory, America, 2015" is featured as an Instagram Micro Essay on the *Creative Nonfiction* website.

There are too many to thank who have loved me through difficult times, who have made my life as a writer possible, and who have challenged or guided me immeasurably. I hope you know who you are.

But special gratitude goes to the man who didn't run when any reasonable person might have, who stayed until things got better. For my sweet and unwavering husband, Keith Shelton, thank you times googolplex, plus infinity, and forever—or at least until death.

VINE LEAVES PRESS

Enjoyed this book?
Go to *vineleavespress.com* to find more.

CPSIA information can be obtained
at www.ICGtesting.com
Printed in the USA
BVOW11s0759300717
490584BV00002B/31/P